The Victorians

John Malam

HODDER
Wayland

an imprint of Hodder Children's Books

THE PAST *in pictures*

Titles in this series ✹ The Victorians ✹ The Home Front

Editor: Elizabeth Gogerly
Original Design: Roger Hammond/Joyce Chester
Designer: Joyce Chester

First published in 1999 by Wayland Publishers Limited
This edition published in 2002 by Hodder Wayland,
an imprint of Hodder Children's Books
© Hodder Wayland 1999

British Library Cataloguing in Publication Data
Malam, John
The Victorians – (The past in pictures)
1. Great Britain – Social conditions – 19th century -
Pictorial works – Juvenile literature
I.Title
941'. 081

ISBN 07502 2695 1

Typesetter: Joyce Chester
Printed and bound in Hong Kong

To contact the author, John Malam, you can e-mail him at:
johnmalam@aol.com

Picture Acknowledgements
The publishers would like to thank the following for permission to
reproduce their pictures:
© Barnados 13 (bottom); Beamish North of England Open Air
Museum 7 (top), 9 (bottom, right), 24 (right), 25 (bottom, left), 26 (top),
29 (top), 30 (right), 35 (bottom, left), 37 (bottom, left); © Brunel
University 20 (top); © City Museum & Art Gallery, Birmingham 41
(bottom, right); Dennis Day *cover* (background); Mary Evans 5
(bottom), 11 (top), 21, 23 (bottom), 25 (top), 27 (bottom), 29 (bottom),
35 (top), 36 (top), 37 (top), 40 (left & right), 43 (top & middle);
© Florence Nightingale Museum 32 (bottom); Getty 5 (top), 18 (left),
26 (bottom),33 (top); © Illustrated London News (*cover*), 5 (bottom), 4
(bottom), 5 (left), 11 (bottom), 25 (right), 42 (bottom); Ironbridge
Gorge Museum Trust 19 (all pictures); John Malam 16 (left & right), 17
(top left, bottom), 18 (right), 33 (left & bottom), 36 (bottom), 37
(middle), 39 (top), 43 (bottom) 44 (second left); © New Scotland Yard
34 (bottom); Robert Opie 4 (top), 27 (top), 29 (middle), 31 (middle), 42
(top); Museum of London 7 (bottom), 12, 15 (bottom, 22 (top), 28, 30
(left); © National Portrait Gallery (*cover*); Peter Newark Military
Pictures 38 (top & bottom); © Norfolk Museum Services 14 (top, left),
32 (top); Popperfoto 8 (bottom), 10, 35 (bottom, right), 38 (middle), 41
(top); Public Record Office 22 (bottom, left), 34 (top); Royal
Photographic Society 9 (top), 20, 39 (bottom), 41 (bottom, left);
© Science Museum (*cover*), 22, 23 (top), 24 (left); © Tate 31 (bottom)
Wayland 7 (middle), 8, 9 (bottom, left), 13 (top), 14, 15 (top, left), 17
(top, right), 21, 31 (top).

With special thanks to the Ironbridge Gorge Museum Trust for
kind permission to use their photographs in this book.

The Victorians

Contents

The Royal Family

In 1837, an 18-year-old princess became the new Queen of Great Britain and Ireland. Her name was Alexandrina Victoria, and she ruled for 64 years. Queen Victoria married her German cousin, Prince Albert, and they had nine children. The public liked the Royal Family, and crowds came to see them wherever they went.

▼ Souvenirs, like this wooden jigsaw of Queen Victoria's coronation, were made to celebrate important events. Souvenirs were produced in their millions. They were cheap to buy, and the public liked them.

◄ Queen Victoria in her coronation robes in 1838. On her head is the Imperial State Crown, sparkling with 3,250 diamonds and other precious stones. She holds the Sceptre with the Cross, which stands for power and justice. On the fourth finger of her right hand is the Coronation Ring, also called the Wedding Ring of England.

◄ Queen Victoria said that Prince Albert was 'quite charming' and 'handsome'. He worked hard and helped Victoria to do her job.

❝ My Dearest Cousin,
Now you are Queen of the mightiest land of Europe;
in your hand lies the happiness of millions …
I hope that your reign may be very long, happy,
and glorious. ❞

PART OF A LETTER WRITTEN TO
QUEEN VICTORIA IN 1837, BY PRINCE ALBERT

► When the Royal Family was in London, they lived in Buckingham Palace. Victoria never really liked it, she said it was a cold house. Her favourite home was Osborne House, on the Isle of Wight.

Towns

During Queen Victoria's long reign, millions of people left the countryside to live in towns, where they worked in factories and shops. By 1900, most people in Britain lived in towns. They were busy places. The streets were crowded with horse-drawn carriages, delivery vans, bicycles, and trams, and the first cars had begun to appear.

▲ Shopkeepers displayed their goods on stands outside their shops, or suspended them from poles above the pavement. Victorian shops were quite small and they were usually owned by families who lived above them.

◄ Fleet Street in London, in 1885. Horse-drawn carts and carriages pack this major road. Note how many of the vehicles have advertising signs on them. In the background St Paul's Cathedral can be seen.

◄ Workmen called night soil men had the unpleasant job of removing sewage ('night soil') from people's outside toilets, which they took away in carts. In the 1840s towns started to build underground sewers to take sewage away.

◄ Houses for working people were often built in unsuitable places. Here, rows, or terraces, of houses have been built next to a noisy, smoky railway viaduct. A narrow passage divides one row from another. It was along passages like this that the night soil man came.

► By the 1840s, town streets were lit by gas. Lamp-lighters had the job of lighting and putting out every lamp by hand. By the end of the century, electric lights had started to replace gas lights.

Agriculture and the Countryside

The 'golden age' for agriculture was between 1840 and 1870. Farmers began to use new types of machinery to help them with their work. Wet land was drained so that more crops could be grown, and fertilizer was spread over the fields to improve the soil.

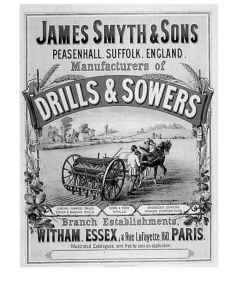

▲ Many Victorian farm machines were powered by horses. Manufacturers advertised their machines on posters like this.

> 66 Success to the farmer,
> The plough and flail,
> May the landlord ever flourish,
> And the tenant never fail. 99
>
> A TRADITIONAL HARVEST RHYME

◄ At harvest time, gangs of labourers went from farm to farm to cut fields of corn. The ears of wheat or barley were taken to the farmyard to be threshed, and the hay stalks were left in the fields to dry. In this photograph women use pitchforks to lift the hay onto a horse-drawn wagon. Hay fed the farm's animals in winter.

▶ Machines powered by steam changed the way farms worked. This photograph, from 1860, shows a steam engine supplying power to a thresher. The thresher shook the stalks of wheat or barley to make the grains of corn fall out.

▼ Farm workers lived in cottages on the farms where they worked. They were the tenants of the farmer, and he was their landlord. They paid him rent. In this cartoon from a Victorian magazine, a farmer and his wife are visiting a cottage. The cottage has just one room and a family of seven live there. The farmer's wife is not used to seeing such poverty.

▼ Every town and every village had one or more blacksmiths. A blacksmith made things from iron, which he heated up in the fire of a forge until it was soft enough to knock into shape with a hammer. Blacksmiths, like the man in this picture, made horseshoes and tools.

People – the Middle and Upper Class

Victorian society was divided into groups, called the upper, middle, and lower classes. Everyone fitted in to a group, depending on how wealthy they were, whether they owned land, and what sort of work they did. Middle class people worked for their money. Many of them owned factories. They were the 'newly rich'. Upper class people inherited money and land from their families. They were the 'old rich'.

◄ This middle class family is in their drawing-room at home in the 1890s. The room is large and well-decorated. There are pictures, rugs, curtains, and the furniture is well-made. Everyone is dressed in their best clothes. Photographs like this show us the comfortable lifestyle which many Victorian families enjoyed.

◀ Many members of the upper class belonged to hunting clubs. Foxes, stags, hares and birds were hunted in Victorian Britain.

▼ The upper class enjoyed the best things in life. This painting shows a group of people at the end of a dinner party. Servants brought the food to the table and a butler was in charge of the wine. These guests are dressed for the occasion: the men in dinner jackets and bow ties, and the women in elegant dresses and jewellery.

66 Aunt Catherine and I write or sew until eleven. Uncle Richard goes shooting with Sir Charles Cuyler. In the evening we form a very cheerful party by the drawing-room fire, reading, or sewing, or playing games. 99

WRITTEN IN 1851 BY ANNA MARIA FAY, AN AMERICAN VISITING HER WEALTHY UNCLE IN ENGLAND

People – the Lower Class

Most people belonged to the lower class. In this group were people who worked in factories and in the countryside. Most lived in houses owned by landlords, to whom they paid rent. But there were many people who were out of work and who lived rough on the streets.

▼ The poorest people of all were the destitute. Some were ill, most were old, and none of them worked. Workhouses were built all over the country to house them. They were large, unpleasant, overcrowded places. By the end of the 1800s, some workhouses had become orphanages and hospitals.

◄ The poverty of this family is easy to see. Their small room is both a workroom and a bedroom. The parents and three of their children make toys to sell in the street and at fairs. Perhaps this was the only way the family could earn a living.

▼ Many people were forced to live on the streets and some families abandoned their children. In 1868, Thomas Barnardo, known to everyone as 'Dr Barnardo', opened the first of his homes for homeless children. By 1900, more than 60,000 homeless boys and girls, like the boy in this picture, had been rescued from the streets. Dr Barnardo's homes gave them food and shelter.

❝ No destitute child ever refused. ❞

SIGN OUTSIDE EVERY Dr BARNARDO'S HOME FOR HOMELESS CHILDREN

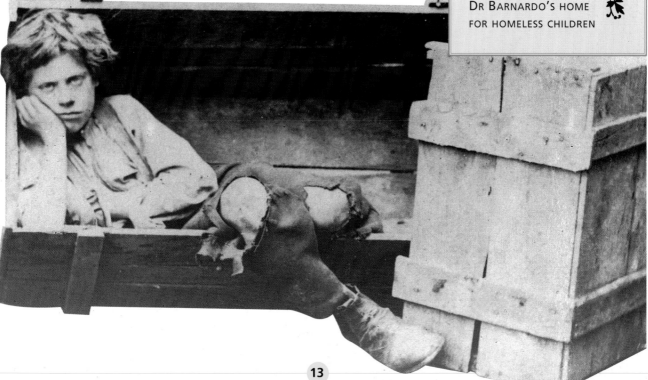

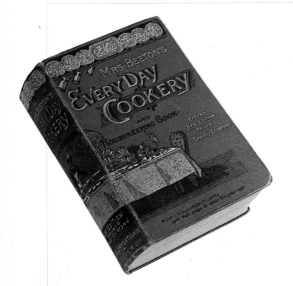

Food

In towns, servants did the shopping and cooking for middle and upper class families. People in these classes ate good food. Every day they had fresh fruit and vegetables, and meat. People in the lower class ate meat only two or three times a week, and sometimes only on Sundays. The poorest people could not afford any meat. They lived on cheese, bread, porridge, and potatoes.

▲ In 1861, Isabella Beeton wrote a book called *Book of Household Management*. It was full of good advice and tips on everything needed to run a home, from cooking meals to the duty of servants. Such was the success of the book that Mrs Beeton wrote many other books, like the one seen above.

► Two of the biggest chocolate manufacturers in Britain in the 1800s were Fry's and Cadbury's. Both produced bars of eating chocolate from the 1840s. Adverts like this appeared in magazines. The boy in the middle is letting his friend have a bite of his chocolate.

◄ Horse-drawn dairy carts were a familiar sight in many towns, bringing fresh milk, butter, and cheese to the homes of the middle and upper classes. Here, a milkman is delivering the day's milk to a household maid.

One of the biggest problems in the kitchen was keeping food cool, to prevent it from going bad too soon. The Victorians had several ways of doing this, one of which was by using a cool box, like the one seen here. A layer of ice was packed into the bottom of the box, and the food was placed on top of it. With the lid shut, the food stayed fresh until needed for cooking. ▶

In London, Covent Garden was the city's main fruit and vegetable market. Traders arrived early each day to set up their stalls. Customers came from all over the city to buy potatoes, carrots, cabbages, onions, apples, pears – and many other fresh goods. It was a busy place to work and shop. This picture was painted in 1864. ▼

66 Onions emit so very disagreeable an odour that no truly polite person will eat them when liable to inflict their fumes upon others. 99

ADVICE GIVEN IN THE 1880S, IN A BOOK CALLED *HOW TO BEHAVE: A POCKET MANUAL OF ETIQUETTE AND GUIDE TO CORRECT PERSONAL HABITS*

Clothes People Wore

When a woman wanted a dress, or a man wanted a jacket, a dressmaker or a tailor made one for them. Fashions came and went. From the 1860s, clothes became more colourful than before as new dyes came into use. Children's clothes were smaller versions of adult's clothes.

▼ Manufacturers invented some unusual items of clothing, such as corsets for women and belts for men which used magnetism to improve the shape of the person's figure. Not only that, the makers claimed they cured sleeplessness and loss of appetite!

▲ A couple dressed in their best clothes in the 1860s. The woman wears a crinoline dress, and her husband a plain jacket over a striped waistcoat and trousers. He is carrying a pocket watch on a long chain. It is tucked into his waistcoat pocket.

THE "VERY THING" FOR LADIES
FOR AN ELEGANT FIGURE & GOOD HEALTH
HARNESS' MAGNETIC CORSETS
PRICE ONLY 5/6 POST FREE
THEY CURE WEAK BACK.
FOR WOMEN OF ALL AGES
HARNESS' MAGNETIC CORSETS
ONLY 5/6 POST FREE
By wearing these perfectly designed Corsets the most awkward figure become graceful and elegant, the internal organs are speedily strengthened.
THE CHEST IS AIDED IN ITS HEALTHY DEVELOPMENT.
And the entire system is invigorated.
Send at once Postal Order or Cheque for 5s. 6d. to the Secretary, C Dept.
THE MEDICAL BATTERY CO., LIMITED.
52, OXFORD St LONDON. W.
ONLY 5/6 POST FREE

▲ Fashionable gentlemen wore top hats. They were made in many styles – see page 20 for a very tall top hat.

▲ Women's day dresses in the 1870s were straight at the front, with a short train behind. This woman is probably wearing a corset under her dress to squeeze her waist in. Hats were always worn when going outside.

66 In towns, it should be the aim of every nice woman to avoid attracting attention by her dress, manner, or style. Reds, bright blues, pinks, and vivid greens are among the colours that should be avoided in town costume. 99

ADVICE GIVEN TO GIRLS IN THE 1880S, IN A BOOK CALLED *THE YOUNG LADIES' TREASURE BOOK*

► Under this woman's crinoline dress of the 1860s is a framework of cane or steel hoops, tied to her waist. Her dress falls over the frame, giving it this distinctive, bell shape.

Buildings

Victorian architects and designers built some of the most distinctive buildings Britain has ever seen. During Victoria's reign, railway stations were built in towns all over the country. Churches were built in the latest style of architecture; bridges spanned rivers once thought impossible to cross; and huge buildings housed exhibitions to entertain the public.

▼ As towns grew, new churches were built, and many old ones were restored. This is Temple Church in London which was restored in the 1840s in an ornate style known as Gothic Revival.

◄ Grand buildings were often built at the ends of railway lines. This building at St Pancras Station was built in the 1860s.

◄ On 1 May 1851, Queen Victoria opened the Great Exhibition, held in Hyde Park, London. It was a display of more than 100,000 different objects, from pieces of furniture to industrial machines.

> ❝ It was neither crystal nor a palace. It was a bazaar, admirably constructed for its purpose. ❞
>
> **LEIGH HUNT (1784–1859), POET**
> THIS IS HOW HE DESCRIBED THE CRYSTAL PALACE

► People travelled from all over to visit the Great Exhibition. It was housed inside a building made from iron and glass. The building was called the Crystal Palace.

◄ Building the Forth Bridge, across the Firth of Forth in Scotland. The first trains crossed it in 1890. At the time, it was the biggest bridge in the world.

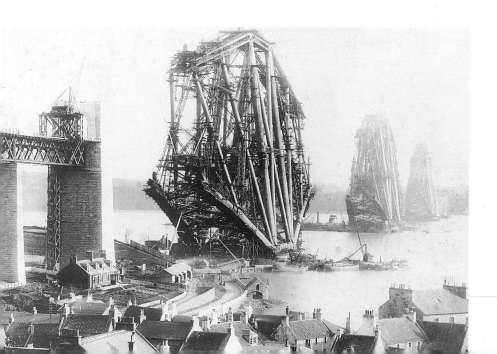

Industry and Engineering

Britain became the leading industrial country in the world during Queen Victoria's reign. It was an age of machines and factories. Machines did the work that was once done by hand, and even bigger factories were built for them. Towns such as Manchester, Leeds, and Birmingham grew into major industrial centres.

▲ Isambard Kingdom Brunel (1806–59) was the greatest of all Victorian engineers. He built bridges, railway lines and huge ships powered by steam. This photograph shows Brunel standing in front of the chains used to launch his ship the *Great Eastern.*

❝ Houses are interspersed with blazing furnaces, heaps of burning coal, piles of ironstone, forges, pit-banks, and engine chimneys… small remaining patches of the surface soil are occupied with irregular fields of grass or corn, intermingled with heaps of the refuse of mines or slag from the blast furnaces. ❞

AN 1843 DESCRIPTION OF THE LAND AROUND WOLVERHAMPTON IN THE WEST MIDLANDS

◀ Victorian towns were unplanned – factories and warehouses sprang up wherever there was land. In this photograph you can see the textile mills of Leeds, with their tall, sooty chimneys, standing next to houses.

◀ By the middle of the 1800s, iron-making had become one of the country's great industries. In this painting, a steam hammer is about to crash down onto a bar of red-hot iron. Iron was used to make items such as nails, chains, fireplaces, fountains, statues, and ships.

One of the last great feats of civil engineering in the Victorian period was the construction of the Manchester Ship Canal in the 1890s. It was dug by navvies, or navigators. They dug a 35-mile long ditch to join Manchester to the sea. Ships sailed up and down the canal, bringing in cotton from America, and taking cloth out. ▼

Transport

The transport system underwent great changes in the Victorian period. Railways took over from canals to become the most important form of land transport, taking people and goods to all parts of the country. By the end of the period, a new transport revolution was on its way, as the first motorized vehicles had started to appear.

▲ For most of the Victorian period, carriages pulled by horses were the main means of transport around towns. They were called cabriolets, or cabs. A favourite type of cab was the hansom cab, invented in 1834 by Joseph Hansom. The driver sat high up at the back and spoke to his passengers through a small door in the roof.

Railway companies issued timetables showing the times at which their trains ran each day. ▼

From the 1830s, railways grew in importance. Steam-powered locomotives travelled faster than canal boats and coaches – by the 1890s, speeds of 60mph (95kph) were common. Trains brought fresh goods into towns. They were also used for pleasure, taking people from towns on day trips to the seaside. ▼

The Victorians had many different types of bicycle. One type, seen here, was the high bicycle, or ordinary. Because it had a large and a small wheel, it was nicknamed the 'penny-farthing' after two coins – a penny (which was large) and a farthing (which was small). Its pedals were fixed to the big wheel. It was hard to start, and as there were no brakes it was difficult to stop. ▶

> 66 It was declared that the railway would prevent cows grazing and hens laying. The poisoned air from the locomotive would kill birds as they flew over them. 99

SOME PEOPLE WERE AGAINST RAILWAYS. THIS IS WHAT SAMUEL SMILES, AN AUTHOR, SAID

◀ In the 1890s, the first motor cars appeared on the roads of Britain. Until 1896 the Government said they could not travel faster than 4mph (6.5kph). In 1896 the law was changed, and cars were allowed to travel at faster speeds.

Discoveries

The Victorians were curious about the world around them, and there were many questions they wanted answers to. For instance, scientists wondered where human beings had come from. Others tried to unravel the secret of flight. New ways of making better quality products were found. It was a time of great discovery, especially in science.

▼ Throughout the 1800s, attempts were made to conquer the air, most notably by balloons filled with hydrogen or coal gas. Most balloon ascents were done in the name of science. Other flights, like the one you can see here, entertained people at fairs.

▲ Cartoonists dreamt up weird-looking flying machines, like the ones seen here. They imagined that one day people would fly in machines that flapped their wings, just like birds. But in reality, Victorian flying machines were little more than gliders.

◄ Iron was used to make railway rails, ships' hulls, bridges, and parts for machines. In 1856, Henry Bessemer discovered how to convert iron into steel by forcing air through molten iron to burn out impurities. The end result was a much harder and more useful metal than iron.

Charles Darwin was a doctor who became interested in natural history. He discovered how animals evolved from other animals. His book, *On the Origin of Species by Means of Natural Selection* (1859), upset many people who believed the Bible story of creation. However, Darwin's theory about how life developed remains one of the great discoveries of the Victorian period. ►

◄ Coal was the most important fuel in the Victorian period. In some coal mines a gas oozed from the coal seams. The gas caused explosions which killed hundreds of miners every year. A chemist, Humphrey Davy, found out what this gas was. This discovery led to the invention of the miner's safety lamp, which warned miners if this dangerous gas was in their mine.

❝ What can be more curious than that the hand of a man, formed for grasping, and the wing of a bat, should be constructed on the same pattern, and should include the same bones, in the same relative positions? ❞

CHARLES DARWIN (1809–82)
SCIENTIST AND NATURALIST

Inventions

The Victorian period was a time of rapid change. Inventors found ways of making new machines and new processes which affected everyone's life. The telephone was a new method of communication, the first photographs were taken, typewriters clattered away in offices, and at night, towns glowed with light shining from electric lamps.

▲ The first photographs were taken in Britain in the 1830s. People visited studios to have their photographs taken. Street photographers, such as the one seen here in the 1870s, worked from portable studios. You can see some photographs mounted on his stall.

▲ In 1877, the American inventor Thomas Edison made the first recording of a human voice. He called his talking machine the phonograph. In 1888, Emile Berliner found a way of recording sounds on to discs, and so the gramophone was born. By the end of the century, upper class Victorian parlours everywhere were filled with the crackly sounds of the gramophone.

► Two inventors, Joseph Swan, in Britain, and Thomas Edison, working in America, discovered how electricity could be used to provide a constant source of light. Edison's lamp was the more successful of the two inventions. From the 1880s onwards, electric lamps were used to light streets, factories, public buildings, and houses.

> 66 No. 9 on from 1.30 am till 3 pm (13½ hours) then cracked glass and busted. 99
>
> **THOMAS ALVA EDISON (1847–1931),** INVENTOR, EDISON WROTE THIS IN 1879, FOLLOWING AN EXPERIMENT WITH AN ELECTRIC LIGHT

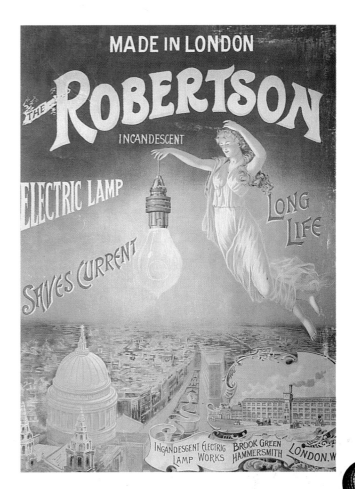

◄ On 10 March 1876, the Scottish inventor Alexander Graham Bell uttered the famous words to his assistant: 'Come here, Watson, I want you.' The two men were in different rooms, and Bell's voice was sent along a wire. It was the world's first telephone call. His invention was a great success. In 1878, Queen Victoria spoke by telephone for the first time at Osborne House.

Leisure and Entertainment

Longer working hours meant less time for leisure and entertainment. However, some sports, such as football, tennis, and cricket, became an important part of the weekly timetable for many people. They played or watched them in what little spare time they had. Some forms of 'entertainment', such as cockfighting, went out of fashion and died out.

▼ A summer's day in Hyde Park, London in 1858. As towns grew, parks were formed where people could relax in their leisure time. For people who lived and worked in the industrial cities, the town parks were often as close to being in the countryside as they could get.

► Prize fighting was rough and tumble. There were no rules, and contestants fought with bare fists. In 1867 the Marquis of Queensbury wrote a set of rules. Out of these came the sport of boxing. Many men still preferred prize fights like the one in this picture.

66 Lawn tennis is all that a pastime for men and women should be. It is an outdoor game; it is pleasant to play at, and pleasant to see played; and there is room in the game for almost any degree of skill and judgment, strength and activity. 99

TAKEN FROM *THE YOUNG LADIES' TREASURE BOOK*, OF THE 1880s

A form of tennis had been played for several hundred years before the modern game appeared in the 1870s. It became extremely popular with the middle and upper classes. This advertisement for tennis equipment shows a game of mixed-doubles. ►

◄ Indoor entertainment, particularly for the lower and middle classes, might have meant a visit to the music hall. These were theatres where the 'pop-stars' of the time entertained audiences with their songs and the audience sang along. Music halls put on many other types of variety act, such as juggling and comedy.

A Trip to the Seaside

In the first years of the Victorian period, trips to the seaside were enjoyed mainly by the wealthy upper class. They could afford to travel long distances by stage-coach. But when railways were built, everything changed. Lower class people from the industrial cities could afford to go on trips to the coast. Seaside towns, such as Aberystwyth, Blackpool, Brighton and Scarborough, grew into major holiday resorts.

▼ These children are playing in the sand on Seaton beach, north-east England. Behind the children are bathing wagons, inside which bathers changed into their swimming costumes.

◀ Puppet shows, such as Punch and Judy, were popular at the seaside. Booths, which looked like tiny theatres, were pitched on the beach, and crowds gathered to watch the fun.

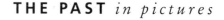

◄ Every major resort had a pier. It was a long iron structure which stretched out above the sea. These children are under a pier in Brighton and there is another pier in the background.

► Gifts from the seaside became popular, such as small pieces of china decorated with a picture of the resort. The jug seen here shows the pier at Southsea.

> 66 I am a Bug, a seaside Bug,
> When folks in bed are lying snug,
> About their skin we crawl and creep,
> And feast upon them while they sleep,
> In lodging-houses, where we breed,
> And at this season largely feed. 99
>
> A VICTORIAN RHYME

► This painting of Ramsgate Sands shows how the Victorians kept themselves covered, to keep the sun off their skin. It was unfashionable for anyone to get a suntan then.

Public Health

In the 1830s, towns were unhealthy places to live. Diseases, such as cholera, spread quickly due to dirty conditions and overcrowding. By the end of the 1800s, housing had been improved, rubbish and sewage were collected, and drinking water was free of germs.

▲ Inside this wooden chest are some of the things used by a Victorian chemist to make different medicines. The glass jars contain powders and liquids, and the drawers hold dried plants and pots of ointment.

▼ During the Crimean War Florence Nightingale had nursed wounded soldiers and had felt angry about how the sick men were treated. After the war, in 1860, she opened the Nightingale School of Nursing at St Thomas's Hospital in London. Women came here to train as nurses. This picture, taken in 1866 shows Florence surrounded by some of the country's first nurses.

> 66 The first aim of a hospital should be to do the sick no harm. 99
>
> **FLORENCE NIGHTINGALE (1820–1910), NURSE**

► This photograph shows two nurses working on a hospital ward for women. Florence Nightingale insisted that wards were neat and tidy, bed linen was clean, and there were spaces between beds. You can see here that her rules have been followed.

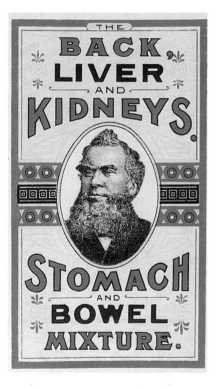

► A nurse in the 1880s. Nurses dressed in smart, clean uniforms. Hanging from this nurse's waist are two pairs of scissors, a pair of forceps, and a watch. She would have used these in her daily work.

▲ The Victorians tried to make remedies for everything. But medicines didn't always do what they said on the label. Some manufacturers made exaggerated claims for their medicines.

Crime and Punishment

As towns grew, the amount of crime increased. There were pickpockets on the streets, and burglars broke into shops and houses. Murders were committed, too. New jails were built to house the growing numbers of people sent to prison. Many, such as Pentonville prison in London, had cells for more than 500 inmates. A prisoner's life was made as hard as possible.

▼ The first police force in Britain was in London, created in 1829 by Sir Robert Peel. Their headquarters were at Scotland Yard, seen here in the buildings they occupied until 1890. Other towns followed London's example and set up their own police forces of 'Peelers', as they were known.

▲ This photograph shows two men arrested for murder. Murder was a capital offence, which meant the punishment was death by hanging. Until 1868, criminals could still be transported to other countries.

◀ The exercise yard at Newgate Prison, London in the 1870s. In 1878 a prison system was set up with the slogan 'hard bed, hard fare, hard labour'. For the first part of a sentence, prisoners were locked up alone. They slept on wooden planks and they were not allowed books.

The Victorians believed that work cured a prisoner's life of crime. They worked long hours, from 6 in the morning to 7 at night. This photograph shows prisoners at Dartmoor prison. They are inside a workshop sewing mail sacks for the Post Office. ▼

Police officers carried short wooden sticks, called truncheons, which they used against anyone resisting arrest. When an officer retired, he kept his truncheon, decorated with his initials and the badge of his police force. ▼

Children

Most Victorian families had five or more children. Children from rich families ate well, wore good clothes, had toys, and nannies looked after them. Children from poor families had few, if any, of these things. For them, life could be cruel and short. The Government stopped children from working in mines and factories, and free education was made available to them all.

▲ By the end of the Victorian period, all children between the ages of 5 and 13 had to go to school, where they were taught reading, writing, arithmetic, history, geography, and physical education. The children in this photograph are from lower class families.

▼ Boys from upper class families were sent away to be educated at public schools. Their parents paid for their education. Note how the boys are wearing school uniform, and their teachers are dressed in gowns and hats.

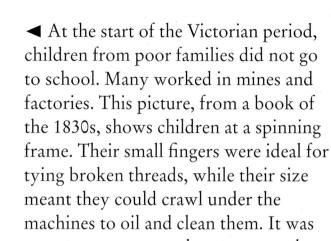

◄ At the start of the Victorian period, children from poor families did not go to school. Many worked in mines and factories. This picture, from a book of the 1830s, shows children at a spinning frame. Their small fingers were ideal for tying broken threads, while their size meant they could crawl under the machines to oil and clean them. It was dangerous work, and accidents often happened. Children who did not work hard enough were beaten like this boy.

❝ I don't know how old I am; don't know how long I have been to work; don't know how long I have been a mould runner; don't know if I got a birthday. I can't read, I can't write, I never had no schooling. I come [to work] at five or six [in the morning], go home at nine [at night]. ❞

LEVI TAYLOR, A FACTORY WORKER, AGED ABOUT **12** IN 1841

▼ For many poor Victorian children, the only place to play was in the street. This group of lower class children are dressed in poor quality clothes which are little better than rags. Three of them do not have shoes on their feet.

▲ Children from wealthy families enjoyed riding three-wheeled cycles. Here, a brother and sister proudly show off their expensive machines.

37

Britain at War

In 1854, Britain and France took Turkey's side in a war against Russia. It was fought in a part of Russia called the Crimea. After three years, Russia was defeated, but 22,000 British soldiers had died in battle or of disease. In the 1880s and 1890s, Britain fought Dutch settlers, called Boers, in South Africa. The Boers were defeated, but the war made problems for South Africa's future.

▲ An army officer's hat from the 1850s. British army officers wore smart uniforms. This hat, called a shako, was worn in the Crimean War.

▲ The Crimean War (1854–1856) was the first war in history to be photographed. It was also the first war in which reporters used the telegraph to send eyewitness stories back to their newspaper offices. In this photograph, soldiers are seen at rest, away from the battlefield.

▼ In 1856, a new medal was given to some soldiers who had fought in the Crimean War. It was called the Victoria Cross and it was only awarded to men who had been very brave.

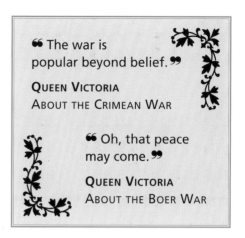

◄ The three stripes on the sleeves of this soldier's uniform show that he has the rank of sergeant in the British army. This photograph was taken in the 1870s.

▼ The final war of the Victorian period was the Boer War (1899–1902), fought in South Africa. Soldiers wore khaki uniforms for the first time. Uniforms in this earthy colour camouflaged the soldiers, which made it hard for the enemy to see them.

Government and Empire

Britain ruled countries all over the world. They belonged to the British Empire. At its height, the countries of the Empire covered one-quarter of the Earth's surface. Thousands of people began new lives in Britain's colonies overseas, and more than half a million left Britain in the 1880s alone.

◀ William Gladstone (1809–1898) was Liberal prime minister four times during Queen Victoria's reign. The upper class did not trust him because they feared he wanted to take away some of their powers. He worked hard to improve life for the less privileged people in society. In 1870, his government passed a law which made education available to all young children.

▲ The countries, or colonies, of the British Empire are shown in red. They provided Britain with food, and with raw materials such as cotton and rubber. British factories turned them into finished goods, which were sold all over the world. Britain's Empire helped to make her a leading nation.

◄ In 1861, Prince Albert died. Queen Victoria was heartbroken and she went into mourning. She was not seen in public for a long time. After many years, Benjamin Disraeli, the Prime Minister, encouraged her to begin some public duties again. In 1876, his government gave her the title Empress of India. It was a way of saying she was the Queen of India too.

▼ This picture, called *The Last of England*, was painted by Ford Madox Brown in 1855. It shows emigrants sailing to a new life in a British colony. Emigrants moved to countries in the British Empire, such as Australia, Canada and New Zealand.

► Benjamin Disraeli (1804–1881) was Conservative prime minister two times during Queen Victoria's reign. The Queen supported him in his work to expand the British Empire. In 1875, his government passed a law which allowed town councils to pull down the worst houses, or slums, and replace them with good quality homes.

❝ I have singled out a couple from the middle classes, high enough, through education and refinement, to appreciate all they are giving up. ❞

FORD MADOX BROWN (1821–1893), ARTIST, WRITING ABOUT HIS PAINTING *THE LAST OF ENGLAND*

End of an Era

Victoria was Queen for 64 years. No king or queen before her had ruled Britain for such a long time. For most people, she was the only monarch they had ever known – only the elderly could remember Britain before Victoria was queen. Victoria died in 1901, aged 81. The Victorian era died with her.

66 As the carriage passed the Palace-gates, the first great shout of welcome went up. On the one hand the sea of eager human faces, the kaleidoscope colours of ladies' dresses, the brilliant uniforms, the waving hats and handkerchiefs; on the other the happy Sovereign, looking every inch a Queen, and bowing with a gracious dignity as the roars of acclamation met her. 99

ALFRED E. KNIGHT, AUTHOR.
DESCRIBING THE DIAMOND
JUBILEE PROCESSION,
22 JUNE 1897

▲ In 1887, Queen Victoria celebrated her Golden Jubilee. She had been Queen for 50 years. Ten years later, in 1897, she celebrated her Diamond Jubilee. By then she had been Queen for 60 years. Each occasion was marked by a grand procession in London, and in towns all over Britain parties were held in the streets. People bought jubilee souvenirs, such as this plate which showed the British Empire.

◄ Through the marriages of her children and grandchildren, Victoria was related to the royal families of Germany, Norway, Russia, Greece, Sweden, Romania, and Spain. She had 40 grandchildren, and 37 great-grandchildren, and she was affectionately called the Grandmother of Europe.

◄ Queen Victoria died at Osborne House, her home on the Isle of Wight. She lay in state there for ten days. Her eldest son, the new King, Edward VII, placed a diamond crown on the coffin. At each corner was a soldier of the Grenadier Guards. They stood with their backs to the coffin, their heads bowed, and with their rifles held upside-down.

► From the Isle of Wight, the Queen's coffin was taken by boat and train to London. At Victoria Station it was placed on a gun-carriage. Thousands of mourners from Britain, and the British Empire, lined the streets to watch it pass. From London, it was taken to St George's Chapel, Windsor, and in a private family service she was buried next to her husband, Albert.

◄ Cards, edged in black as a sign of mourning, were printed in their millions. They reminded people of the beloved Queen they had just lost.

Timeline of the

1819	Princess Alexandrina Victoria was born
1837	Queen Victoria came to the throne
1838	Queen Victoria's coronation
1838	A gardener from Buckinghamshire became the first living person to be photographed
1840	Queen Victoria married her German cousin, Albert
1840	Postage stamps were first used
1840s	Railway boom in Britain
1842	Women and girls, and boys under 10, were banned from working in mines
1843	The first Christmas cards were sent
1845–48	A potato famine in Ireland killed one million people
1847	Discovery of chloroform
1851	The Great Exhibition was held in London
1851	The first free public library was opened, in Winchester
1853	Vaccination against smallpox was made compulsory
1854–56	Crimean War fought by Britain and France against Russia
1854	Florence Nightingale cared for wounded soldiers in the Crimean War
1856	The Victoria Cross medal was first awarded for bravery in battle
1856	Every town had to have a police force
1858	Launch of Brunel's steamship *the Great Eastern*

Victorians

1857–58	There was an uprising in India against British rule there
1859	Charles Darwin wrote *The Origin of Species*
1861	Prince Albert died from typhoid
1864	Boys under 10 banned from climbing inside chimneys to clean them
1865	Discovery of antiseptics
1868	Disraeli became Prime Minister for the first time
1868–74	Gladstone became Prime Minister for the first time
1868	The 'boneshaker' bicycle was invented
1870	Education made available to every child
1872	First Football Association Cup Final
1874–80	Disraeli became Prime Minister for the second time
1876	Queen Victoria became Empress of India
1876	Invention of the telephone
1878	Electricity first used for street lights, in London
1887	Queen Victoria celebrated her Golden Jubilee – 50 years as queen
1895	The first motor-car factory was opened, in Birmingham
1896	Communication by radio waves made possible
1897	Queen Victoria celebrated her Diamond Jubilee – 60 years as queen
1899–1902	The Boer War was fought in South Africa
1901	Queen Victoria died, aged 81

Glossary

Blacksmith A person who works with iron in a forge.

British Empire Countries in all parts of the world that were ruled by Britain.

Cholera A dangerous infectious disease.

Class A group of people with many things in common.

Colony A country ruled by another country.

Coronation The ceremony at which a person is crowned king or queen.

Crinoline A bell-shaped dress worn over a framework of hoops.

Destitute Having no money at all nor other means of support.

Emigration Moving away to start a new life in another country.

Forge The workshop where a blacksmith works.

Glider An aeroplane which floats, or glides, through the air.

Gramophone A machine for playing sounds recorded onto discs.

Lamp-lighter A person who lit street lamps.

Locomotive A railway engine.

Lower class The worst-off people. They had little money, lived in slums, did the worst jobs, and could not read or write.

Middle class A new class of people in the Victorian Age. They ran businesses, owned factories, were well educated, and earned money for themselves through hard work.

Music-hall A theatre where entertainers performed to audiences.

Navvies Labourers who did heavy outdoor work, such as the men who built railways.

Night soil The contents of toilets, water closets, privies, and cesspits.

Ordinary A type of bicycle with a large and small wheel. Also known as a penny-farthing.

Peeler A policeman.

Phonograph A machine for playing sounds recorded onto cylinders.

Pier An iron, wood, and stone structure built out to sea.

Servants People who work for others in their own homes, such as cooks and maids.

Sewers Underground pipes and tunnels which helped to clean up towns by carrying waste matter and dirty water away.

Slums The worst type of housing, usually in the centre of a town, lived in by the poorest people.

Soot A black deposit made by coal-burning fires.

Terminus The end point of a railway line.

Terrace A row of houses joined together.

Thresher A machine for hitting corn to release the grains.

Transported When a criminal was sent to live in another country.

Tricycle A cycle with three wheels.

Truncheon A policeman's wooden staff or stick.

Upper class The best-off people. They owned land, had a lot of money, and did not need to work for their living.

Viaduct A bridge that carries a road or a railway.

Workhouse A place where poor people did unpaid work in return for food and shelter.

Further Information

Books to read

The Victorians, by Peter Hicks (Wayland, 1995)

Victorians, by Ann Kramer (Dorling Kindersley, 1998)

Victorian Britain 1837–1901, by Andrew Langley (Hamlyn, 1994)

History Starts Here: The Victorians, by John Malam (Wayland, 1999)

The Victorian Years, by Margaret Sharman (Evans, 1995)

Places to visit

MONUMENTS

Albert Memorial, London
The national memorial to Prince Albert.

Victoria Monument, London
The national memorial to Queen Victoria.

ROYAL HOMES

Balmoral Castle, Scotland
Victoria's home, used by today's Royal Family. Some rooms are open to the public.

Buckingham Palace, London
Victoria's London home. Some rooms are open to the public.

Holyrood Palace, Edinburgh
The home of the kings of Scotland. Contains a display of objects linked with Queen Victoria.

Osborne House, Isle of Wight
Some rooms have been left just as they were when Victoria died here in 1901.

SELECTED MUSEUMS

North of England Open Air Museum
Co. Durham (phone: 01207 231811)
An open air museum with reassembled authentic buildings, recreating the history of Northern England during the 19th and early 20th centuries.

Black Country Living Museum
Dudley (phone: 0121 557 9643)
An open air museum with reassembled authentic buildings in a canalside setting, recreating the history of the industrial West Midlands.

Museum of Science and Industry in Manchester
Manchester (phone: 0161 273 2244)
Displays of engineering and transport, the world's oldest passenger railway station (1830), and a reconstructed length of Victorian sewer for visitors to walk through.

Ironbridge Gorge Museum
Shropshire (phone: 01952 433522)
An open air museum at Blists Hill recreates a 19th century village of the Shropshire coalfield, with demonstrations of Victorian processes.

Index

Numbers in **bold** refer to pictures as well as text.